Creating a Thankful Heart Bible Study

By Lorie Eubank

Unveiling True Wealth: The Power of Gratitude

Gratitude is a virtue that holds immense spiritual and psychological significance. It is the act of recognizing and appreciating the blessings and goodness in our lives, whether big or small. Throughout the Bible, we find numerous references to the importance of thankfulness.

In this "Creating a Thankful Heart Bible Study," we will go on a journey through scriptures, exploring the multifaceted dimensions of gratitude. By reflecting on biblical narratives, verses, and teachings, we will work to cultivate an enduring spirit of thankfulness, grounding our lives in a profound appreciation for God's unwavering love and the abundant blessings that punctuate our existence.

May this book serve as an anchor for your heart, guiding you toward a deeper understanding and practice of gratitude and drawing you closer to the heart of God.

Gratitude as an Act of Worship

Gratitude is not merely a casual expression of politeness; it is an act of worship that acknowledges God's sovereignty and provision. The Bible instructs us to offer thanksgiving as a sacrifice to God:

Psalm 50:14-15 (NKJV) - "Offer to God thanksgiving, and pay your vows to the Most High. Call upon me in the day of trouble; I will deliver you, and you shall glorify Me."

Our gratitude reflects our dependence on God and demonstrates our willingness to honor and glorify Him. Through thanksgiving, we acknowledge God's role as our provider and sustainer.

Are there blessings in your life
that you often overlook because
they seem ordinary?

Gratitude in All Circumstances

Being thankful is not contingent on favorable circumstances alone. The Bible teaches us to give thanks in all situations, even in the midst of trials and challenges:

1 Thessalonians 5:16-18 (NKJV) - "Rejoice always, pray without ceasing, in everything give thanks; for this is the will of God in Christ Jesus for you."

James 1:2-3 (NKJV) - "My brethren, count it all joy when ye fall into various trials, knowing that the testing of your faith produces patience."

These verses remind us that even during difficulties, gratitude should be our response. A heart full of gratitude can transform adversity into opportunities for growth and spiritual development.

How can you become more intentional about recognizing and thanking God for all of the blessings in your life?

Gratitude for Salvation

The pinnacle of God's love and grace is manifested in the gift of salvation through Jesus Christ. Our response to this remarkable gift should be unceasing gratitude:

2 Corinthians 9:15 (KJV) - "Thanks be unto God for his unspeakable gift."

Salvation, in all its glory, is the ultimate reason for our thanksgiving. It stands as a testament to the depth of God's love and the boundless extent of His grace. Through the sacrifice of Christ, we are offered a path to redemption, forgiveness, and the promise of eternal life. It is a gift that reshapes our destiny, cleanses our souls, and bridges the gap between humanity and divinity.

When we reflect on the concept of salvation, we uncover layers of gratitude that extend far beyond mere words. It is an overwhelming gratitude that encompasses the realization of our own unworthiness and the sheer magnitude of God's mercy. It is a gratitude that acknowledges the depth of our sins and the immeasurable price paid by Christ on the cross. It is a gratitude that propels us to our knees in humble reverence and heartfelt thanksgiving.

Reflect on the profound concept of salvation through Jesus Christ and the unceasing gratitude it inspires. Explore your personal journey of faith and how the gift of salvation has impacted your life.

Gratitude for God's Abundant Blessings

The Bible is replete with references to God's abundant blessings in our lives. From the air we breathe to the relationships we cherish, we are encouraged to acknowledge God's goodness:

Psalm 103:2 (KJV) - "Bless the Lord, O my soul, and forget not all his benefits."

James 1:17 (KJV) - "Every good gift and every perfect gift is from above, and cometh down from the Father of lights, with whom is no variableness, neither shadow of turning."

Recognizing and being thankful for these blessings shifts our perspective from what we lack to what we have received. Gratitude fosters contentment and prevents us from taking God's gifts for granted.

When you think about your current
life circumstances, can you
identify areas or situations that
are challenging to express
gratitude for?

Gratitude as a Reflection of God's Character

God's nature is characterized by love, compassion, and mercy. As His children, we are called to emulate these qualities, including gratitude:

Colossians 3:15 (KJV) - "And let the peace of God rule in your hearts, to the which also ye are called in one body; and be ye thankful."

Ephesians 5:20 (KJV) - "Giving thanks always for all things unto God and the Father in the name of our Lord Jesus Christ."

Our gratitude not only honors God but also reflects His character to the world. It demonstrates our willingness to be transformed by His love and grace.

How does cultivating gratitude affect your decision-making process, especially when faced with significant choices or challenging situations?

Gratitude and Contentment

In a fast-paced world where materialism and constant comparison often dominate our thoughts and actions, gratitude emerges as a powerful antidote, guiding us toward a place of deep contentment and fulfillment. This invaluable wisdom is beautifully encapsulated in 1 Timothy 6:6 (KJV): "But godliness with contentment is great gain."

In a society that continually bombards us with messages of needing more, aspiring to greater wealth, and measuring success by material possessions, the concept of contentment might seem elusive. Yet, the Bible's teaching reminds us that true wealth is not measured by the accumulation of worldly goods, but by the state of our hearts and our relationship with God.

At its core, gratitude is an acknowledgment of blessings received, whether big or small, and an expression of thankfulness for the abundance that surrounds us. It encourages us to pause and reflect on the blessings we often take for granted —health, love, family, friendships, and the very breath in our lungs.

Think about how your understanding of
gratitude and contentment shapes your
goals for the future. How do you
envision living a life characterized by
godliness, contentment, and a heart
full of gratitude?

Gratitude and Healing

Thanksgiving is linked to physical, emotional, and spiritual well-being. Expressing gratitude has been shown to alleviate stress, improve mood, and enhance overall health. The Bible's wisdom on this matter is profound:

Proverbs 17:22 (KJV) - "A merry heart doeth good like a medicine: but a broken spirit drieth the bones."

When we cultivate a thankful heart, we contribute to our own holistic well-being.

Gratitude is not just a fleeting sentiment; it is a way of life that honors God, shapes our character, and brings about profound inner peace. As we meditate on these scriptures and allow their truths to penetrate our hearts, may we be inspired to live lives characterized by thankfulness in every circumstance.

Consider the quote from Proverbs 17:22, and write about how practicing gratitude has affected your physical, emotional, and spiritual health.

9 Things That Hinder You From Being Thankful And
How To Overcome Them

Gratitude is a transformative attitude that can bring joy, perspective, and a sense of contentment to our lives. However, in the hustle and bustle of our daily routines, we often find ourselves struggling to maintain a thankful heart.

1. Comparison: The Thief of Joy

In a world fueled by social media, comparison is a relentless enemy of gratitude. When we constantly measure our lives against others' seemingly perfect moments, we lose sight of our own blessings.

When we compare ourselves to others, we can become envious or dissatisfied, forgetting the blessings we already have. In Galatians 6:4 (NLT), the Bible instructs, "Pay careful attention to your own work, for then you will get the satisfaction of a job well done, and you won't need to compare yourself to anyone else."

Overcoming comparison: Focus on God's unique plan and purpose for your life. Count your blessings and practice contentment (Philippians 4:11-13). When you feel the urge to compare, shift your focus to gratitude for the blessings you have.

Do you find yourself comparing your blessings to those of others, sometimes leading to envy or ingratitude?

2. Busyness: The Barrier to Reflection

Life's often frantic pace leaves us with
little time for reflection. When we're
constantly on the move, we overlook the small
moments that warrant gratitude.

Slowing down and taking time to reflect on the
simple joys, like a beautiful sunset or a
heartfelt conversation, can rekindle your
thankfulness.

Explore the concept of slowing down. What are
some strategies or practices you can implement
to create space for reflection and gratitude
in your life? How might these practices
enhance your overall well-being?

Taking time to take care of ourselves is an
investment worthy of your time. Slow down and
give thanks for these moments as you sit in
His presence.

How has your understanding of gratitude grown from when you first started your faith journey? How has it changed over time?

3. Entitlement: The Enemy of Appreciation

The feeling of entitlement can creep into our minds, making us believe that we deserve everything without a second thought. This mentality diminishes our appreciation for the blessings we have.

Deuteronomy 8:18 (NIV) "Remember the LORD your God, for it is He who gives you the ability to produce wealth, and so confirms His covenant, which He swore to your ancestors, as it is today."

In this verse, the Israelites were reminded not to forget the Lord or think that their own power and might have earned them their wealth. It's a call against pride and self-sufficiency, pointing out that it is God who equips and blesses. It encourages a posture of gratitude and humility rather than a sense of entitlement.

Write about a time when you felt particularly grateful for a blessing in your life. How can you cultivate a mindset of gratitude and humility in your daily life to counteract feelings of entitlement?

4. Negative Focus: Dwelling on the Disheartening

It's easy to get caught up in negativity, especially when challenges arise. Focusing on problems rather than solutions or dwelling on what's going wrong can obscure the many things that are going right.

Philippians 4:8 (NIV) "Finally, brothers and sisters, whatever is true, whatever is noble, whatever is right, whatever is pure, whatever is lovely, whatever is admirable—if anything is excellent or praiseworthy—think about such things."

Challenge yourself to shift your focus by intentionally finding positives in every situation, no matter how small they may seem.

Challenge yourself to find one positive aspect in a current challenge or difficult situation you are facing. How can this shift in focus help you maintain a more optimistic mindset?

5. Complacency: The Comfort Zone

When life becomes routine, we often slip into complacency, taking our blessings for granted. We stop noticing the everyday wonders that once brought us joy.

Ephesians 5:15-17 (NLT) So be careful how you live. Don't live like fools, but like those who are wise. Make the most of every opportunity in these evil days. Don't act thoughtlessly, but understand what the Lord wants you to do

To break free from this roadblock, embrace a mindset of curiosity and awe. Approach each day with fresh eyes, actively seeking out moments and reasons to be thankful.

What are some practical steps you
can take to break free from
complacency and rediscover the joy
in life's simple pleasures?

6. Pride: The Power of Me

Biblical perspective: Pride can make us feel self-sufficient, leading us to think we don't need God or others.

In Proverbs 16:18, the Bible says, "Pride goes before destruction, a haughty spirit before a fall."

Overcoming pride: Recognize that everything we have comes from God (James 1:17). Cultivate humility by frequently reflecting on God's grace and acknowledging our dependency on Him.

Regular prayer, confession, and worship can help maintain a humble heart.

Explore ways to overcome pride and cultivate humility, as suggested in James 1:17. Describe how regularly reflecting on God's grace and acknowledging your dependency on Him can help you maintain a humble heart.

7. Worry or Anxiety

Worry can cloud our view of God's provision
and care.

Philippians 4:6-7 says, "Do not be anxious
about anything, but in every situation, by
prayer and petition, with thanksgiving,
present your requests to God. And the peace of
God, which transcends all understanding, will
guard your hearts and your minds in Christ
Jesus."

To overcoming worry, cast all your anxieties
on God, trusting in His promises and
providence. Regularly practice prayer and
thanksgiving to shift your focus from worry to
gratitude.

Reflect on the idea that the peace of God can guard your heart and mind in Christ Jesus. How can this promise serve as a source of comfort and strength in times of anxiety?

8. Materialism

When we prioritize material possessions or worldly success, we can forget the more significant spiritual blessings.

1 Timothy 6:10 warns, "For the love of money is a root of all kinds of evil."

We need to overcoming materialism and realign our priorities by focusing on eternal treasures rather than temporary ones (Matthew 6:19-21).

Generosity and acts of service can also help detach our hearts from material things and grow in gratitude for spiritual blessings.

Share a personal experience where giving or serving others increased your gratitude for spiritual blessings. How does the act of serving others help you maintain a thankful heart?

9. Unforgiveness

Holding onto anger or resentment can hinder our grateful heart.

Ephesians 4:32 (NLT) reminds us, "Instead, be kind to each other, tenderhearted, forgiving one another, just as God in Christ forgave you."

Reflect on God's forgiveness towards us, which can motivate us to forgive others. Releasing bitterness and forgiving others can free our hearts to experience gratitude more fully.

Challenge yourself to explore the concept of releasing bitterness and embracing forgiveness as a means of freeing your heart to experience gratitude more fully.

How can forgiveness help you let go
of negative emotions and create
space for gratitude and healing in
your life?

10 Practical Ways To Create A Thankful Heart In Your Everyday Life

Start and End Your Day with Thankfulness:

The Power of Routine: Just as we have routines for brushing our teeth or having a meal, establishing a habit of gratitude at the beginning and end of the day anchors our mind to a posture of thankfulness. By making this a regular practice, we condition our minds over time to default to gratitude.

Setting the Tone: Starting your day with a thankful heart sets a positive tone for the day ahead. This initial act of gratitude can act as a buffer against stress, negativity, or unforeseen challenges that might come your way. When you begin with appreciation for what you have and the day's potential, you're better equipped to handle its ups and downs.

Reflection and Perspective: Ending your day with thankfulness allows for reflection. No matter how challenging or mundane the day seemed, finding aspects to be grateful for can shift our perspective from what might have gone wrong or what we lack, to appreciating the gifts, experiences, and interactions that enriched our day.

Deepening Connection with God: These moments of gratitude create a deeper relationship with God. By consistently acknowledging His hand in the day-to-day blessings and challenges, you nurture a continuous dialogue with Him, recognizing His active role in your life.

Emotional and Mental Well-being: Numerous studies have indicated the positive effects of gratitude on emotional and mental health. By focusing on blessings rather than shortcomings, you cultivate a more optimistic and content outlook on life, which contributes to overall well-being.

Encourage Others: Share your practice with family or friends. Consider starting and ending group gatherings, dinners, or meetings with moments of shared thankfulness. Not only does this encourage others to adopt a similar habit, but shared expressions of gratitude can deepen relationships and create a collective, positive atmosphere.

In essence, by purposefully starting and
ending each day with gratitude, you're
building a life that not only acknowledges the
blessings, both big and small, but also one
that actively seeks out joy, even in the
simplest of moments. This consistent practice
acts as a foundation, building on the many
reasons to be thankful that might otherwise be
overlooked in the hustle and bustle of daily
life.

How do you envision this practice
benefiting your daily life and
overall outlook? Set a goal of 30
days and see how your overall
outlook improves.

Keep a Gratitude Journal: 

Intentional Reflection: Keeping a gratitude journal requires you to pause and actively reflect on your day. This daily commitment pulls you away from the fast-paced routine and offers a moment to intentionally recognize the blessings, both overt and subtle, in your life.

Shifting Mindset: Over time, the consistent act of jotting down grateful thoughts retrains your brain to seek out and focus on the positive. Instead of dwelling on stressors or challenges, you become more attuned to silver linings and moments of joy, which can significantly improve your overall outlook on life.

Tangible Evidence: On tough days when it seems difficult to find something to be grateful for, flipping through past entries serves as a tangible reminder of the myriad blessings you've experienced. The journal becomes a testament to the continuous presence of God and all of the goodness in your life.

Depth of Appreciation: As you maintain the journal, you might find yourself diving deeper beyond surface-level gratitude. Instead of general statements like "I'm thankful for my family," you might begin to note specific moments, like "I'm grateful for the laughter shared with my sister today" or "Thankful for my child's unexpected hug this morning."

Creativity and Personalization: Your gratitude journal can be as simple or creative as you wish. Some people decorate their journals, include photos, sketches, or even quotes that resonate with them. This personal touch can make the practice even more enjoyable and meaningful.

Fostering Consistency: By setting aside a specific time each day, perhaps just before bed or during a morning routine, you create a habit. This consistency not only strengthens the habit but also provides a predictable time of peace and reflection in your day.

Enhancing Spiritual Connection: The gratitude journal can also serve as a spiritual exercise, deepening the connection with the Lord. It's a space to acknowledge God's hand in the day-to-day, recognizing that every good gift comes from above.

Beneficial for Mental Health: Studies have shown that focusing on gratitude can have a variety of mental health benefits, including reducing symptoms of depression and anxiety. The act of journaling can be therapeutic, and when combined with gratitude, it serves as a powerful tool for well-being.

In conclusion, a gratitude journal is more than just a diary of thankful thoughts. It's a tool that facilitates a deeper appreciation for life's journey, bringing a mindset shift towards positivity, deepening spiritual connections, and promoting mental and emotional well-being. By dedicating time to this practice, you're investing in a holistic approach to cultivating a thankful heart.

Pages are included in the end of the book to allow you to journal 30 days of Thankfulness.

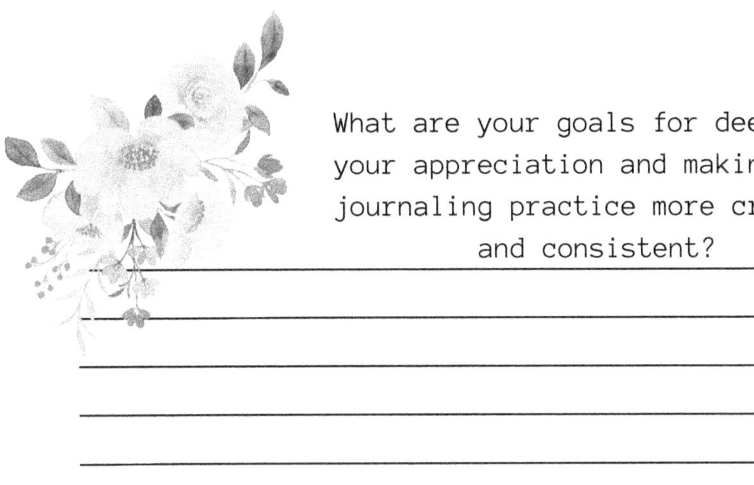

What are your goals for deepening
your appreciation and making your
journaling practice more creative
and consistent?

Express Thankfulness in Relationships:

Strengthening Bonds: Taking the time to express appreciation in relationships reinforces bonds and deepens connections. It makes those around you feel valued and seen, promoting mutual respect and understanding. In a world where many interactions can be transactional, showing genuine gratitude becomes a refreshing and meaningful act.

Promoting Positive Communication: Regularly expressing thankfulness produces a positive communication pattern. By acknowledging the good in others and vocalizing it, you encourage an environment where individuals are more open, supportive, and kind to each other.

Cultivating Emotional Resilience: In challenging times, the habit of expressing gratitude can serve as a buffer against negativity or resentment. Instead of getting mired in misunderstandings or frustrations, focusing on and voicing the positive aspects can help navigate tensions and conflicts.

Encouraging Reciprocity: When you show
appreciation, it often encourages a reciprocal
response. This isn't to say gratitude should
be expressed with the expectation of receiving
something in return, but it naturally boosts
an environment where thankfulness becomes a
shared sentiment.

Boosting Self-awareness: Taking moments to
express gratitude requires introspection. It
challenges individuals to reflect on what they
truly value in their relationships and
interactions. This heightened self-awareness
can lead to personal growth and a better
understanding of one's relationship dynamics.

Memorable Gestures: A heartfelt thank-you
note, a simple message, or even a small
gesture like making a cup of coffee can be
deeply touching. These acts, though seemingly
small, are often remembered for a long time
because they resonate with sincerity and
warmth.

Building Trust: When people know they are appreciated, they are more likely to trust and open up. By regularly expressing gratitude, you're not just acknowledging someone's worth but also building layers of trust, which is foundational in any relationship.

Setting a Positive Example: Particularly in environments like workplaces or homes with children, expressing gratitude can set a positive example. It offers a model behavior that others, especially younger ones, can emulate, thereby perpetuating a culture of appreciation.

In essence, expressing thankfulness in relationships isn't just about acknowledging the good deeds or qualities of others; it's a multi-faceted practice that nurtures relationships, creates positive environments, and contributes to personal and communal well-being. By choosing to be intentional in showing appreciation, individuals can deeply enrich their connections with others, making every interaction a potential moment of gratitude and connection.

Consider the role of gratitude in setting a positive example, in your workplace or with younger individuals in your life. Have you witnessed or practiced gratitude as a model behavior?

Practice Mindful Thankfulness:

Presence in the Moment: In our fast-paced world, it's easy to get caught up in our thoughts, plans, and worries. Mindful thankfulness requires one to be fully present, observing the here and now without judgment. By intentionally pausing and appreciating the present moment, we become more attuned to the richness of life that's often overlooked.

Connecting with Creation: Taking the time to appreciate nature and the world around us can be a profound spiritual experience. By acknowledging the beauty of a sunset, the intricate design of a leaf, or the melody of bird songs, we not only appreciate God's artistry but also feel more connected to the divine tapestry of life. This intentional recognition amplifies our appreciation of God as the Master Creator.

Mental and Emotional Well-being: Being mindful and present has been linked to numerous mental and emotional benefits. When we tune into the present and focus on gratitude, it can reduce feelings of stress, anxiety, and overwhelm. It's a reminder that amidst life's complexities, there are simple moments of beauty and joy to be found.

Cultivating A Continuous Dialogue with God: By thanking God for His creation regularly, we foster a continuous and intimate dialogue with Him. It's a reminder that He's always near, evident in every detail around us. This practice can deepen one's spiritual connection and reliance on God.

Enhancing Sensory Appreciation: Practicing mindful thankfulness engages all senses. Whether it's feeling the texture of a petal, hearing the rustle of leaves, seeing the vastness of the night sky, or smelling the freshness after rain, each sensory experience becomes an avenue for gratitude.

Counteracting Negative Bias: The human brain has a tendency to focus on negatives, a trait inherited from our ancestors who needed to be alert to potential threats. By consciously practicing mindful thankfulness, we can counteract this natural bias, training our minds to seek out and revel in positive experiences.

Promoting Humility: Pausing to appreciate the vastness and intricacies of creation can evoke feelings of humility. Recognizing our smallness in the grand scheme of things, and yet understanding God's immense love and attention to detail, can be both humbling and uplifting.

In essence, practicing mindful thankfulness isn't just a fleeting moment of gratitude; it's a transformative habit that impacts one's spiritual, mental, and emotional dimensions. By making it a point to pause, reflect, and thank God for the everyday wonders around us, we anchor ourselves in a continuous state of appreciation, drawing closer to God and finding joy in the mundane and the magnificent.

Explore the practice of mindful thankfulness and its potential to enhance your connection with the present moment and your overall well-being.

Turn Complaints into Thankfulness:

Shifting Perspective: Our perspective plays a crucial role in how we perceive and react to situations. When faced with adversity, it's easy to focus solely on the negative aspects. However, by actively seeking the silver lining, we choose to view challenges as opportunities for growth, lessons to be learned, or blessings in disguise.

Building Resilience: Turning complaints into thankfulness helps cultivate resilience. By finding reasons to be grateful even in trying times, we equip ourselves to bounce back from setbacks more effectively. Over time, this positive approach not only strengthens our emotional and mental fortitude but also deepens our faith and trust in God's plan for our lives.

Strengthening Character: This practice refines our character. Choosing gratitude over complaint develops virtues like patience, perseverance, and humility. It teaches us to be content in all situations, recognizing that even in hardship, there's always something to be thankful for.

Positive Ripple Effect: Our attitude and reactions have a ripple effect on those around us. By embodying an attitude of gratitude, we influence our surroundings positively. Others can be inspired by such an outlook, and it can create a more optimistic and supportive environment, be it at home, in the workplace, or within a community.

Deepening Relationship with God: In every challenge, there's an opportunity to draw closer to God. By seeking reasons to be thankful, we acknowledge God's sovereignty and goodness, even when His plans might seem difficult to understand. This continuous reliance and trust can deepen our spiritual connection and dependence on Him.

Combatting Stress and Anxiety: Chronic complaining can contribute to feelings of stress and anxiety. Conversely, gratitude has been linked to improved mental well-being. By intentionally focusing on thankfulness, we can alleviate some of the emotional burdens associated with challenging situations.

Encouraging Problem-Solving: A mindset that looks for the positive in adversity is also more likely to approach challenges with a problem-solving attitude. Instead of getting bogged down by the issue, gratitude can motivate proactive thinking, prompting us to find solutions or alternative perspectives.

In summary, turning complaints into thankfulness is not about denying or suppressing difficulties but about adopting a more holistic perspective. It's about recognizing that even in the midst of trials, there are blessings to be found, lessons to be learned, and growth to be experienced. By making this shift in perspective a consistent practice, we not only enhance our personal well-being but also enrich our relationships with others and with God.

Reflect on the transformative power of turning complaints into thankfulness and how it can shape your perspective, resilience, and character.

Serve Others with Gratitude:

A Cycle of Positivity: Gratitude has a unique way of multiplying when shared. By serving others out of a heart of thankfulness, we not only share our blessings but also amplify our own feelings of gratitude. Seeing the positive impact on someone else's life can deepen our own appreciation for what we have.

Tangible Expression of Thankfulness: Serving is a proactive way to express gratitude. Instead of just feeling thankful, you're putting that emotion into action. Acts of service can be viewed as a tangible "thank you" to God or to those who have blessed you in your own life.

Building Empathy: Engaging in acts of kindness allows us to step into another's shoes, even if just for a moment. This can heighten our sense of empathy, making us more attuned to the blessings in our lives and the struggles others face. Recognizing these contrasts can deepen our own feelings of gratitude.

Enriched Relationships: Serving others often leads to enriched interpersonal relationships. These genuine interactions, based on selflessness and gratitude, can create bonds of trust, understanding, and mutual respect. Through service, we often discover a shared humanity that fosters deeper connections.

Holistic Personal Growth: Acts of service contribute to personal growth in numerous ways. Beyond cultivating gratitude, they teach patience, humility, and compassion. This holistic development enhances one's overall character and outlook on life.

Spiritual Fulfillment: For many, serving others is not just a social responsibility but a spiritual calling. Engaging in acts of service can deepen one's connection with God, understanding it as a form of worship and a tangible expression of faith. By serving others, we emulate divine love and generosity.

Breaking the Bubble of Self-Centeredness: In a world that often promotes individualism and self-focus, acts of service help break the bubble of self-centeredness. They remind us of the broader community and our interconnectedness, encouraging a mindset that values collective well-being.

Reinforcing the Value of Non-material Blessings: While serving, we often encounter people who, despite having fewer material possessions, exhibit immense joy, resilience, and contentment. Such encounters can be powerful reminders that the most profound sources of gratitude are often non-material.

In essence, serving others with gratitude is a transformative practice that benefits both the giver and the receiver. It's a practical way to channel one's thankfulness into positive change, leaving lasting impacts on individuals and communities. By choosing to serve from a place of gratitude, we embrace a life that's rich in purpose, connection, and genuine joy.

Reflect on the idea of serving others with gratitude and how it can create a cycle of positivity, provide a tangible expression of thankfulness, and build empathy.

Celebrate Progress:

Acknowledgment of Effort: Celebrating progress, whether major milestones or small achievements, is a way of acknowledging the effort, commitment, and dedication that went into reaching that point. It's a testament to perseverance, hard work, and resilience. When we take a moment to recognize these efforts, we infuse our journey with a sense of meaning and purpose.

Building Self-Worth: Every celebration, no matter how minor the achievement might seem, reinforces a sense of self-worth and competence. It reminds us of our capabilities and our potential. Over time, this consistent recognition boosts self-confidence and self-esteem.

Fueling Forward Momentum: Recognizing and being grateful for progress can act as a powerful motivator. It provides a positive reinforcement loop, where celebrating one achievement fuels the desire and motivation to pursue the next. It creates an upward spiral of ambition, effort, achievement, and celebration.

Creating Joyful Memories: Taking time to celebrate turns moments of progress into joyful memories. These become cherished stories of growth and transformation, acting as reminders of the journey undertaken and the challenges overcome.

Shared Celebrations Amplify Gratitude: Sharing these moments of celebration with friends, family, or colleagues amplifies feelings of gratitude. When others join in our joy and recognize our progress, it fills us with a sense of communal achievement and strengthens bonds.

Grounding in the Present: Celebrating progress is also a way of grounding oneself in the present moment. It's easy to get caught up in future goals or past setbacks. Taking time to be grateful for the present journey and its milestones brings a balance to our perspective on time.

Combatting Burnout: In long and challenging journeys, especially where goals are distant or complex, it's easy to feel overwhelmed or burnt out. Regularly celebrating progress provides necessary pauses of rejuvenation, breaking the journey into manageable and rewarding chunks.

Spiritual Reflection: From a spiritual perspective, celebrating progress can be seen as an act of thankfulness to God for the strength, guidance, and opportunities provided. It's a moment to acknowledge not just personal effort but divine grace that played a role in the journey.

Cultivating a Growth Mindset: Celebrating progress, even the minor steps, reinforces a growth mindset - the belief that abilities and success can be developed through dedication and hard work. This mindset values effort as a path to mastery and learning, and celebrating progress strengthens this belief system.

In summary, celebrating progress is an act of gratitude that carries profound benefits. It's more than just marking a milestone; it's an acknowledgment of the journey, the growth, and the myriad forces - internal and external - that contributed to that progress. By consistently recognizing and celebrating achievements, we nourish our spirit, fortify our motivation, and cultivate a thankful heart that values every step of the journey.

Reflect on the practice of celebrating progress over perfection, and how it can acknowledge effort, build self-worth, and fuel forward momentum in your life.

Turn Gratitude into Action:

Transforming Inner Feelings into Tangible Deeds: Gratitude, while profoundly transformative as an internal feeling, reaches its full potential when translated into actions. By actively seeking ways to express our thankfulness, we not only reinforce our own feelings of gratitude but also create a positive impact in the world around us.

Acts of Kindness: One of the simplest yet most profound ways to express gratitude is through spontaneous acts of kindness. Whether it's buying a coffee for a stranger, helping a neighbor with their chores, or just sharing a warm smile, these gestures, fueled by a grateful heart, contribute to a positive atmosphere and uplift others.

Paying It Forward: Recognizing the blessings and kindnesses we've received, we can adopt a "pay it forward" approach. This could mean mentoring someone as we've been mentored, donating to causes that resonate with our own stories, or simply being there for someone as others have been there for us. In doing so, we create a chain of positivity and gratitude.

Being a Beacon of Encouragement: Armed with a perspective that recognizes blessings, we can be sources of encouragement for others. Our words, actions, and presence can become pillars of support for those who might be going through challenging times, guiding them towards finding their own reasons for gratitude.

Investing in Community: Our feelings of gratitude can inspire us to contribute to our communities, whether it's through volunteer work, starting community initiatives, or supporting local businesses and endeavors. By giving back to the community, we tangibly express our thankfulness for the environment and the people who have played a role in our lives.

Mindful Consumption and Generosity: Gratitude for what we have can guide our consumption habits, making us more conscious of waste and excess. Additionally, it can lead to greater generosity, as we might feel inspired to share our resources, be it time, money, or skills, with those in need.

Building Bridges: A heart full of gratitude is more likely to seek connection over division. With this mindset, we can actively work towards building bridges of understanding, tolerance, and

unity, turning gratitude into a powerful tool for social cohesion and harmony.

Deepening Spiritual Practice: For many, gratitude is deeply intertwined with their faith. Turning gratitude into action can mean deepening one's spiritual practices, seeking a closer connection with the divine, and acting in ways that reflect spiritual teachings of love, compassion, and service.

Personal Growth and Learning: Being grateful for experiences, even the challenging ones, can motivate us to learn and grow continuously. This gratitude-driven growth ensures that we not only better ourselves but also have more to offer to the world in terms of wisdom, skills, and understanding.

In essence, turning gratitude into action is the embodiment of the saying, "actions speak louder than words." While feeling thankful is a profound inner experience, expressing that gratitude through tangible actions magnifies its impact, creating ripples of positivity and change in the broader world. It's a beautiful cycle where gratitude inspires action, which in turn generates more reasons for gratitude.

Can you recall a specific moment
when expressing gratitude
transformed a difficult situation
into a moment of growth or learning
for you?

What Makes Me Happy

What Makes Me Grateful

Why I Should Be Grateful

30 days of Thankfulness

Day 1

Day 2

Day 3

Day 4

30 days of Thankfulness

Day 5

Day 6

Day 7

Day 8

30 days of Thankfulness

Day 9

Day 10

Day 11

Day 12

30 days of Thankfulness

Day 13

Day 14

Day 15

Day 16

30 days of Thankfulness

Day 17

Day 18

Day 19

Day 20

30 days of Thankfulness

Day 21

Day 22

Day 23

Day 24

30 days of Thankfulness

Day 25

Day 26

Day 27

Day 28

30 days of Thankfulness

Day 29

**Day 30

Congratulations on embarking on this journey of
gratitude and thankfulness over the past 30 days
or however many days you have dedicated to it.
Your commitment to cultivating a grateful heart
is a beautiful and transformative endeavor.

Remember that gratitude is not just a 30-day
challenge; it's a lifelong practice that can
continue to enrich your life in countless ways.
By recognizing and appreciating the blessings,
both big and small, you open yourself up to a
world of positivity, joy, and connection.

As you move forward, consider integrating
gratitude into your daily life as a habit.
Continue to seek out moments of thankfulness,
express your appreciation to those around you,
and nurture the sense of contentment that comes
from recognizing the beauty in the world.

Gratitude is a gift you give yourself and
others, and it has the power to transform not
only your perspective but also the world around
you. Keep on this path of thankfulness, and may
it bring you a lifetime of fulfillment and joy.

Creating a Thankful Heart Bible Study